C000257986

i LOVE you

sourcebooks
casablanca

Originally published in the United Kingdom in 2013 by Summersdale
Publishers Ltd.

Published by Sourcebooks Casablanca, an imprint of Sourcebooks, Inc.
P.O. Box 4410, Naperville, Illinois 60567-4410
(630) 961-3900
Fax: (630) 961-2168
www.sourcebooks.com

Printed and bound in China.
LEO 10 9 8 7 6 5 4 3 2 1

TO. . . . .

FROM. . . . .

What force **IS MORE** potent than **LOVE?**

IGOR STRAVINSKY

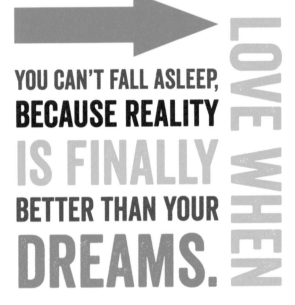

YOU KNOW YOU'RE IN LOVE WHEN YOU CAN'T FALL ASLEEP, **BECAUSE REALITY** IS FINALLY BETTER THAN YOUR DREAMS.

DR. SEUSS

Eventually you will come
to understand that love
heals everything, and
love is all there is.

GARY ZUKAV

We love because
it's the only
true adventure.

NIKKI GIOVANNI

★ ★ ★

THE WORLD IS TOO
DANGEROUS FOR ANYTHING
BUT TRUTH AND TOO SMALL
FOR ANYTHING BUT LOVE.

★ ★ ★

WILLIAM SLOANE COFFIN

THERE IS A
TIME FOR
AND A
TIME

WORK.

FOR LOVE.

THAT LEAVES NO OTHER TIME.

COCO CHANEL

If you press me to say
why I loved him, I can
say no more than because
he was he, and I was I.

MICHEL DE MONTAIGNE

Talk not of wasted affection;

AFFECTI♥N

never was wasted.

HENRY WADSWORTH LONGFELLOW

LOVE IS LIKE
dew that falls on both nettles
AND LILIES.

SWEDISH PROVERB

In dreams and in love there
are no impossibilities.

JÁNOS ARANY

I have spread my dreams
under your feet;
Tread softly because you
tread on my dreams.
W. B. YEATS, "HE WISHES FOR THE
CLOTHS OF HEAVEN"

Love is like pi—natural, irrational, and very

IMPORTANT.

LISA HOFFMAN

Falling in love
CONSISTS
merely in uncorking the
IMAGINATION
and bottling the
COMMON SENSE.

HELEN ROWLAND

Love is not altogether
a delirium, yet it
has many points in
common therewith.

THOMAS CARLYLE

I want to do with
you what spring does
with cherry trees.

PABLO NERUDA

LOVE IS A GAME THAT TWO CAN PLAY AND BOTH WIN.

EVA GABOR

IN THE SPRING A YOUNG
MAN'S FANCY LIGHTLY TURNS
TO THOUGHTS OF LOVE.

ALFRED, LORD TENNYSON,
"LOCKSLEY HALL"

To love and be loved
is to feel the sun
from both sides.

DAVID VISCOTT

I should call love a
single pure activity.

D. H. LAWRENCE

LOVE HAS no uttermost, as the stars have no number and the sea no rest.

ELEANOR FARJEON

Love is a
FRIEN♩SHIP
set to music.

E. JOSEPH COSSMAN

To love is to feel one
being in the world at
one with us, our equal
in sin as well as virtue.

EMMUSKA ORCZY

LOVE

MUST

BE AS MUCH A LIGHT AS IT IS A FLAME.

HENRY DAVID THOREAU

What does love feel like?
INCREDIBLE.

REBECCA ADLINGTON

Lust is easy. Love is hard.
Like is most important.

CARL REINER

Love is the answer, but
while you're waiting
for the answer, sex
raises some pretty
good questions.

WOODY ALLEN

Anyone can be
PASSIONATE,
but it takes real lovers
TO BE SILLY.

ROSE FRANKEN

A FLOWER CANNOT

➡️

WITHOUT SUNSHINE,
AND MAN CANNOT

LIVE
WITHOUT
LOVE.

BLOSSOM

MAX MÜLLER

What would men be
without women?
Scarce, sir, mighty scarce.

MARK TWAIN

Kiss me and you will see
how important I am.

SYLVIA PLATH

★ ★ ★

SOUL MEETS SOUL
ON LOVERS' LIPS.

★ ★ ★

PERCY BYSSHE SHELLEY

THE BEST smell in the world is that man that you love.

JENNIFER ANISTON

A kiss is a lovely trick
designed by nature to
stop speech when words
become superfluous.

INGRID BERGMAN

It was not my lips you
kissed, but my soul.

Love is an
IRRESISTI◊LE
desire to be irresistibly desired.

ROBERT FROST

PLATONIC love is love from the **NECK UP.**

THYRA SAMTER WINSLOW

If I know what love is,
it is because of you.

HERMANN HESSE

It's love that brings
people closer.

SUNITA CHOUDHARY

The best thing to
hold onto in life is
EACH OTHER.
AUDREY HEPBURN

IN LOVE, THE PARADOX OCCURS THAT

TWO

BECOME

BEINGS
ONE
AND YET REMAIN TWO.

ERICH FROMM

I like to believe that love is a reciprocal thing, that it can't really be felt, truly, by one.

SEAN PENN

A LIFE ➡ WITHOUT LOVE IS LIKE A YEAR WITHOUT SUMMER.

SWEDISH PROVERB

★ ★ ★

LOVE IS COMPOSED
OF A SINGLE SOUL
INHABITING TWO BODIES.

★ ★ ★

ARISTOTLE

Love loves to love love.

JAMES JOYCE

Love life and life will love you back. Love people and they will love you back.

ARTHUR RUBINSTEIN

THE LOVE

we give away
is the only
love we keep.

ELBERT HUBBARD

Love can turn the

CO🏠🏠AGE

into a golden palace.

GERMAN PROVERB

When you love someone,
all your saved-up wishes
start coming out.

ELIZABETH BOWEN

Love is the magician
that pulls man out
of his own hat.

BEN HECHT

Love is a canvas furnished
BY NATURE
and embroidered by the
IMAGINATION.

VOLTAIRE

The more I think it over,
the more I feel that there
is nothing more truly
artistic than to love

PEOPLE.

VINCENT VAN GOGH

The art of love...is largely
the art of persistence.

ALBERT ELLIS

Love is the axis and breath of my life. The art I produce is a byproduct.

ANAÏS NIN

Life isn't LONG ENOUGH for love AND ART.

SHE IS THE HEART  THAT STRIKES

THE WHOLE OCTAVE.
AFTER HER ALL
SONGS ARE
POSSIBLE.

RAINER MARIA RILKE

Love is friendship
set on fire.

JEREMY TAYLOR

WHEN I SAW YOU,
I FELL

IN LOVE.

AND YOU SMILED
BECAUSE YOU KNEW.

ARRIGO BOITO

LOVE IS LIKE SMILING

It never fades and is contagious.

ANONYMOUS

What the world really
needs is more love and
less paperwork.

PEARL BAILEY

Love is an exploding cigar
we willingly smoke.

LYNDA BARRY

The love

RECEIVED

is the love that is saved.

EDDIE VEDDER

Love is being stupid
TOGETHER.

PAUL VALÉRY

Let the lover be
disgraceful, crazy,
absent-minded. Someone
sober will worry about
events going badly.
Let the lover be.

RUMI

And yet, to say the truth, reason and love keep little company together nowadays.

WILLIAM SHAKESPEARE, *A MIDSUMMER NIGHT'S DREAM*

It is impossible to love and be

WISE.

FRANCIS BACON

Kisses are
A BETTER
fate than
WISDOM.

E. E. CUMMINGS

In love there are two
things: bodies and words.

JOYCE CAROL OATES

Sometimes the
heart sees what is
invisible to the eye.

H. JACKSON BROWN JR.

A HEART THAT LOVES ➡️ IS ALWAYS YOUNG.

GREEK PROVERB

★ ★ ★

LOVE CONQUERS ALL
THINGS EXCEPT POVERTY
AND TOOTHACHE.

★ ★ ★

MAE WEST

Being deeply loved
by someone gives
you strength, while
loving someone deeply
gives you courage.

LAO TZU

[He is] quite simply my strength and stay.

ELIZABETH II

THREE THINGS can't be hidden: coughing, poverty, and love.

YIDDISH PROVERB

LOVE IS NOT CONSOLATION. IT IS

LIGHT.

FRIEDRICH NIETZSCHE

Each moment of the
happy lover's hour is
worth an age of dull
and common life.

APHRA BEHN

Love is everything it's **CRACKED UP** to be...worth fighting for, **BEING BRAVE** for, risking everything for.

ERICA JONG

I love her, and that's
the beginning of
EVERYTHING.

CHARLES BUKOWSKI

One of the secrets of
life is that all that is
really worth the doing is
what we do for others.

LEWIS CARROLL

A purpose of human life,
no matter who is controlling
it, is to love whoever is
around to be loved.

KURT VONNEGUT

I am in love—
AND, MY GOD,
it's the greatest thing
THAT CAN HAPPEN
to a man.

D. H. LAWRENCE

WHERE LOVE IS CONCERNED, TOO MUCH IS NOT EVEN ENOUGH.

PIERRE BEAUMARCHAIS

Each time that one loves
is the only time one has
ever loved. Difference
of object does not alter
singleness of passion.
It merely intensifies it.

OSCAR WILDE

If you really love
someone and care about
him, you can survive
many difficulties.

IT'S EASY TO FALL IN LOVE.
THE HARD PART IS FINDING
SOMEONE TO CATCH YOU.

BERTRAND RUSSELL

WHERE there is love there is no question.

ALBERT EINSTEIN

There is no remedy for
love but to love more.

HENRY DAVID THOREAU

There is only one
happiness in life, to
love and be loved.

GEORGE SAND